Comeback
KIDS

Comeback KIDS

A POCKET GUIDE TO POST-PANDEMIC PARENTING

JACQUELYN LAZO &
FRANK DEPIETRO, MD, PHD

ISBN 979-8-507-61258-1 (paper)

Edited by Lisa Medders
Book cover design by Cecilia Sorochin
Composition by Lindsay Starr

To my husband, Aaron, who always carries my heart into the sunlight. And to our daughter, Emma Magnolia, who spreads boundless joy wherever she goes.—J. L.

To my wonderful wife, Amy, who is my rock and my inspiration. — F.D.

To caregivers everywhere — we hope this guide makes your journey a little easier.

CONTENTS

PREFACE

WHY WE WROTE THIS BOOK

We recognized early on that the pandemic would most likely have a significant impact on the mental health of children and their families. Our goal was to provide a tangible way for caregivers and kids from all walks of life to communicate and collaborate during a difficult time.

In April 2020, we started inviting some parents and caregivers we knew to have conversations with their kids about their feelings through a short, five-question survey. We also connected with kids (and their parents) to complete our survey by working with the University of Virginia's Multilingual Outreach Volunteer Effort (MOVE) program, nonprofits and community organizations, and through various social media platforms. We completed the survey in October 2020.

Our data gathering was not designed to be a scientific study; it was intended to shed some light on what kids were thinking in a structured, consistent way. We wanted to encourage more families to share these questions with each other as a gateway to better understanding themselves and their families. We hope our survey serves as a jumping-off point for future research.

We chose our survey questions carefully to gather two key pieces of information about children: (1) their thoughts on their feelings and emotions and (2) how they were thinking about their future during a difficult time.

It was important to us to elevate children's voices, which are rarely prioritized in the public sphere. While they may not have years of schooling under their belts and haven't yet earned academic accolades, they know a thing or two. We wanted them to know we were listening, and so were their caregivers.

Here are the five questions we asked:

1. What are three words to describe how you feel right now?
2. When you think about going back out into the world, what things make you nervous or scare you?
3. In what ways have you seen people help each other during quarantine?
4. What are you most excited to do when this is over, or what are you most hopeful about for the future?
5. What do you think we could all do going forward to help make the world a better place once the virus is gone?

Overall, the survey results showed what a significant impact parents' words and behaviors have on their kids, often even more so than many of us realize. A lot of the kids' answers seemed to echo what adults around them might be saying or what they heard on the news or radio or read online. That's a big reason why we started the book with tips for parents on how to manage their own anxiety.

You'll find the survey and some select responses in Appendix A at the back of the book. If you decide to complete the survey with your own kids, it may be interesting to also share some of the survey responses with them as you talk through their answers. Hearing what other kids had to say can be reassuring — showing your child that all feelings are valid, even if they contradict each other, and that there's no right way to feel.

INTRODUCTION

You know your kids or the kids you care for better than anyone else, so how you choose to use the information in this book is entirely up to you. One size never fits all, so this resource is meant to be a flexible roadmap you can tailor to your family's needs.

Our hope is that you can use this guide to help the children in your care bridge the gap between life before and after the pandemic. This resource is for those of you who are concerned about the mental health and well-being of your children and want to learn how you can best support them.

In this guide, you'll find practical, easy-to-understand information you can use to help you through this post-pandemic phase into the next 'new normal.'

We've included:

- checklists at the end of each section,
- red flags to help you know when to seek professional help,
- action steps you can take, and
- advice on where and how to find more support when you need it.

We've made a special point of noting telltale signs throughout that may provide you with enough information to know how and when to seek help from a mental health professional (these include psychiatrists, psychologists, social workers, and other licensed therapists). Seeking therapy for your child can be challenging for many reasons — which is why we've included information at the end of the guide on the basic steps to help you navigate the process more smoothly.

While therapy is an important part of overall treatment, there are many things you can do at home, so we've also given you some basic self-help tools you can put into place immediately that will hopefully provide some relief. Additionally, we've included some meditation and mindfulness resources you may want to look into if you think they may be of help.

MENTAL NOTE

If you are concerned about your or your child's mental health and safety, contact a mental health professional immediately or use one of the resources listed at the back of the book. Reaching out for help is a sign of strength. You don't have to go it alone.

PART I

REFLECT & PROCESS

What we've experienced during the pandemic has left many of us with lingering anxiety, fear, and doubt — even if we've never experienced feelings like these before. It's changed us in unexpected ways, and it's changed our children.

It's natural to worry about how the pandemic has impacted your family, and you're not alone if you're concerned about how you'll cope while supporting them as we all transition into the next 'new normal.'

Most of us also recognize that our kids are worried about a whole lot right now, and as much as we'd like to sit them down and ask them to tell us their deepest, darkest fears, that approach rarely works. Instead, it may put them on the defensive, and they'll think to themselves, *Okay, what's going to lead to the least hassle for me?* or *How do I get back to playing Fortnite?* What you'll get is a filtered version of the truth, not what's really going on.

So how do we get our kids to be honest with us about how they're feeling?

While it may seem counterintuitive, the best way to prepare to help your kids is to help yourself first. By processing and reflecting on what you've been through, you're taking the first step toward setting the stage to help your kids.

MENTAL NOTE

Dealing with small doses of stress is part of life, and it's something many of us have learned how to live with relatively well. Living in an ongoing state of stress for over a year isn't, and it can have a lasting impact on our bodies as well as our minds.

When we're stressed, our muscles naturally tense as a way to protect us from pain or injury. Our heart rate increases, as does our breathing and our blood pressure. Our body begins producing cortisol to help regulate these responses. Cortisol is the body's stress hormone and is often associated with the 'fight-or-flight' instinct people feel when faced with a stressful situation.

While cortisol is helpful in small quantities, if stress continues for a long period of time, it can have detrimental effects on our body, shortening our life span and increasing the likelihood of mental illness. That's why it's critical to take a little time to reflect and process what we've been through and acknowledge the sustained levels of stress we've been under.

It's also vital we recognize and get in touch with how this stress has made us feel. Our feelings aren't going anywhere. If we don't process them, they'll still be there tomorrow. And the day after. It's better to take conscious consideration of them and deal with them rather than have them unconsciously influence our path forward.

MAP IT OUT

Think about it like you're going on a journey. The first thing you need to do is map out how you're going to get where you want to go based on where you are. In this case, where you want to go might be influenced by where you are. Be honest with yourself (and that's hard to do!). If you ignore how the pandemic has affected you and your current situation, you might not be establishing reasonable goals. You might be expecting too much or too little of yourself. And you might not be giving yourself the chance to imagine possibilities beyond the ones you assumed you'd follow before this crisis started.

To begin, you need to establish where you are right now. That starts with tuning in to how you're feeling.

Step 1: Find Your Focus

Find a time when you can think. As easy as it sounds, this can be the hardest part of the process. It requires clearing away any distractions (we're talking about internal and external distractions, such as electronic devices, children, partners, pets, chores). It also means you need to be in a space where you can focus so you can zero in on how you're doing.

You don't need a lot of time for this. Try to check in with yourself for a few minutes ideally every day or when you can fit it in — before everyone wakes up in the morning or right before you go to bed often works well.

 MENTAL NOTE

We tend to live in a reactive state. We go through our day functioning on autopilot and unintentionally distracting ourselves from the moment. And when we're frantic, the lists keep forming in our minds, as do the distractions. The phone rings, the dog barks, someone yells down the hall. We have only so much

cognitive and emotional energy to deal with all of it. Our internal and external distractions often keep us from ruminating about what we can't let go of or what's bothering us.

And most of the time that's completely fine. It's not necessary (or feasible, frankly) to spend countless hours dwelling on how we're thinking and feeling in our day-to-day lives. We don't have time to engage in what's called metacognitive thinking before every action we take.

If we want to understand and process something big that's happened, however, the surest way to get there is to engage in a metacognitive level of thinking. But since it's not something we do regularly, we may need to pause, step out of our normal reactive state, and actively give ourselves permission to tap into it.

That permission will help you ease into a more introspective frame of mind. You may be surprised by how much tension you're carrying. It's like when someone gives you a back or shoulder massage. All of a sudden, you think, Wow, I didn't realize how much I was tensing my body until now. The same goes for your mind.

Step 2: Confront Your Fears

Once you've given yourself the time, space, and permission to think about your own needs, ask yourself how you feel in this moment. What's been on your mind lately?

Whatever you're feeling, take note of it. You may even want to write it down. Give yourself a minute or two to jot down the emotions or thoughts that come up, whether they're words, phrases, or full sentences.

Having trouble thinking of things to write? Try keeping your pen or pencil moving the entire time, even if it means writing a grocery list, gibberish, or the same word over and over. Giving yourself the freedom to creatively free associate can help you be more expressive about your feelings.

Or, consider carrying a notepad or Post-Its with you for a day. Jot down things as they come to mind, or take notes in your phone. Then you'll have a list ready to go for the next step.

If you're more auditory than visual, it might work better for you to say your fears aloud. Or per-haps you want to paint what you're feeling. You can employ whatever process works for you and allows you to take your thoughts, which are less controllable in your mind, and put them where you can see them.

MENTAL NOTE

Emotions and worries can feel vague or infinite. It's much easier to process and tackle them once they're in front of you. It's often calming to be able to see or hear what you're worried about because it becomes concrete. Maybe you thought there were a million things, and in reality you only identify seven. Anxiety often magnifies your feelings, sometimes to a point where they become all-consuming. Worries also lose some of their power when they come out because they can no longer circle endlessly around in your brain.

When you're processing things in your head, the thoughts go through different pathways than if you name what you're feeling. If you say it out loud or write it down, you can hear it or see it, which gives you an alternate avenue to process it then when it's only internal. You're engaging different levels of sensory-related processing that can actually help you get a handle on how you're feeling.

Step 3: Manage Your Mind

Start at the top of your worry list and ask yourself
the following questions:

- · Is this a realistic worry?
- · When I think about this worry, does it
  overwhelm me?
- · Can I act on this worry, or is it out of my control?

 MENTAL NOTE

*This approach to exploring how to process your wor-
ries helps your mind switch from an emotional mode
to a rational mode, which is a useful skill to practice
anytime you're feeling overwhelmed.*

TRIM DOWN YOUR WORRIES

Let's say you have a page or two of worries. That can
feel like a lot. The first thing is to try to see if there
are any duplicates or if you can categorize them so
that you bring it down to a smaller number. That
will make the list less visually overwhelming.

One way to process your worries is to ask yourself a series of simple questions. You can start at
the top or assess the first worry that jumps out at
you on the page or comes to mind.

Ask yourself:

Is this a realistic worry?

This is something called reality testing. It's about figuring out what evidence you have in support of your worry. Have you come to a reasonable conclusion? Is it possible to have a more realistic thought, or is there a more practical way to manage your worry?

Let's say you're a natural introvert, and you're worried about having to socialize again. You can already feel the pressure of having to decide which event to go to, and it makes you anxious.

Your internal narration goes something like this:

I know my friends and family will be annoyed if I agree to do something but then suddenly back out. Another example could be that you're worried your life will go back to being as hectic as it used to be and you won't know how to handle it.

Maybe you're saying to yourself:

Just thinking about our old schedule exhausts me. But if I don't keep up with everything, I'll disappoint my family, friends, and myself.

MENTAL NOTE
Any automatic negative thoughts like these tend to be exaggerated universal generalizations that have a tremendous amount of power. By their very nature, they also close off options. Try to take a step back from your thought. Ask yourself if what you're thinking feels rational.

In the first example, you can challenge your thinking by asking yourself the following questions:

Have my friends and family gotten annoyed if I've had to back out in the past?

Sometimes.

Have they also been understanding?

Mostly.

What's one thing I could do to help them understand where I'm coming from?

I could tell them up front that I'm anxious.

Is it possible they might be more understanding if I do that?

Probably.

Here's how it could play out in the second example:

Will I really feel exhausted all the time?

Probably not.

Have I handled juggling a lot in the past?
For the most part.
Is there anything I can do to make life less hectic?
Well, I can decide to do less at certain points of the year (or month or week) so it doesn't feel quite as overwhelmingly busy.
What's one thing I could choose not to do?
I could not sign up to volunteer for all of the kids' field trips. Maybe I could just pick a few.

DECIDE IF YOUR WORRIES ARE OVERWHELMING YOU

If you still have quite a few worries on your list, see if you can narrow them down to three or four by asking yourself: *When I think about this worry, does it overwhelm me?*

Whether the answer is yes or no, you get to decide how you want to move forward. There aren't any firm and fast rules, so you can make your own. However, be careful if you notice yourself using this as a strategy to avoid processing by continuously reinventing your rules. Try to find rules that work for you and stick with them for a little while to see if you can make progress.

If you start to get overwhelmed by some of the worries you've identified, you may want to set them aside for now. You can tell yourself, *Okay, I'm not going to forget these worries, and I'm not deprioritizing them. I'm just not dealing with them right now so that I can deal with the things I've identified as the most important to me at this moment.* Make a note to deal with these worries later.

 MENTAL NOTE

As you go through this practice, hopefully you'll begin to gain a degree of confidence — maybe even a sense of mastery. You can do this. You can mark worries off of your list! You can process them and make them manageable. Each success will help increase your confidence. And with more confidence, you may even decide at some point that you're able to handle what you think is the biggest worry on your list.

TACKLE UNREALISTIC WORRIES

Now that you've gotten those worries out of your head where you can see them and have separated the unrealistic ones (to deal with now) from the overwhelming ones (to save for later), it's time to act.

Start by saying, *I need to let go of these unrealistic worries*. Because if somewhere inside you're saying, *I better not let go because something bad might happen*, you're not likely to succeed. You have to be willing to admit to yourself that worrying about this unrealistic idea isn't serving you.

If you're still having trouble letting the worry go, ask yourself, *What am I getting out of doing this? Why do I feel driven to do this? Is it just because somehow if I go over it again and again, I'm trying to assume control? Is there a way I can assume control that is more action-oriented and less ruminative?*

It's really about deciding that this pattern and these worries don't belong in your head, that they're not doing you any good. If you feel like you're ready to do something about them, that in and of itself is a positive step that reinforces you emotionally. It gives you a little boost so you can then say, *Look at that. I did that. I labeled my worries. I put them out there. I took a step. Maybe I can take another step.* It's sequential: Every little gain makes the next step easier.

ACT ON YOUR WORRIES

Next, ask yourself, *Can I act on this worry, or is it out of my control?*

Once you've settled on the worry you want to address, think about whether there are specific ways you can tackle your fear by breaking it down. Are there simple actions you can take to make it feel more manageable or to begin to lessen your worry about it?

If you're worried about your kids adjusting to school again, for example, get as much information as you can ahead of time from the school and the teachers. Think through how your child's routines have changed over the past year and help them begin to make small changes so you don't dread getting them up for the bus in the morning or getting everyone to school on time. Planning ahead can help you feel more in control, and it can ease the transition for everyone.

Step 4: Celebrate Small Wins

If you have time later in the week, think back on what you were worried about. Were you able to make some progress on it? If not, what held you back? Could you break that worry down even more or set it aside and go back to the list?

MENTAL NOTE

Offering yourself positive reinforcement helps build that muscle in your brain. It's like going to the gym — the more you lift a certain weight, the more likely you'll be able to increase the weight you can lift over time. The more you're able to make progress on what you sense is doable, the more likely you are to tackle other concerns the same way.

COMMIT TO CHECKING IN

It's easy to go through this exercise once and then consider yourself done, but the more often you do it, the more you're likely to get out of it.

MENTAL NOTE

Committing to checking in with yourself on a regular basis allows you to engage on a metacognitive level of processing instead of a reactive level of processing. It takes practice to get good at it or even feel comfortable doing it. Try to keep in mind that by making a contract with yourself to look inward on a daily basis or as regularly as possible, you are helping yourself as well as your kids.

GIVE YOURSELF A BREAK

Remember, you can take a break and focus on doing something that gets you out of your head whenever you need to. Change where you're sitting, go outside, or maybe even take a walk. Let yourself step away if that's what you need.

Sometimes writing a list of things you're grateful for can help pull you out of your worries. The simple act of allowing yourself to recognize what brings you joy and fills you up can make you feel less bogged down.

MENTAL NOTE

Negative experiences inherently have a very strong impact on us because of the way our brains are designed. We register them more readily, and when we think back, they tend to stick out in our minds, which can make us lose sight of the positive experiences we've had.

Evolutionarily speaking, this is most likely a result of the fact that early humans had to be cognizant of negative situations and threats more than positive ones as a matter of life or death. In other words, holding onto negative experiences is our brain's attempt to keep us safe.

The good news is that we can actively change this response. By making a conscious effort to focus on the positive things in our lives, like being grateful for the people around us and the good things that have happened to us, we can train our minds to overpower some of the negatives and steer our attitude in a more positive direction.

REFLECT & PROCESS CHECKLIST

Why am I doing this again?

- · The best way to prepare to help your kids is to help yourself first. You're setting the stage to help them by understanding your own feelings.
- · Your feelings about what you've been through aren't going anywhere. It's better to take conscious consideration of them by being aware of and dealing with them than having them unconsciously influence your course forward.

❏ Step 1: Find Your Focus

Find time and space to step out of your day-to-day reactive state for a few minutes. Shut out as many distractions as possible, and try to home in on what's happening on the inside.

❏ Step 2: Confront Your Fears

Ask yourself how you feel in this moment. What's been on your mind lately? Take note of whatever you're feeling. You may even want to write it down, talk it out, or draw it. Use whatever process feels best to get your thoughts out of your head and within your field of vision. This will take the abstract worries and make them feel more concrete, which ultimately makes them more manageable.

❏ Step 3: Manage Your Mind

Investigate your worries further. Ask yourself the following
questions:
- Is this a realistic worry?
- When I think about this worry, does it overwhelm
  me?
- Can I act on this worry, or is it out of my control?

❏ Step 4: Celebrate Small Wins

Check back in with yourself when you have time later in
the week to see how you did. Can you think of small steps
you took to make progress on your worry? If not, what kept
you from doing it? Positive reinforcement gives you a sense
of achievement and instills confidence in yourself that
you can continue to make more steps toward your goal.
Whenever you need it, take a break — whether it's going
for a walk, making a gratitude journal, sitting outside in the
sunshine, or doing some mindfulness exercises.

This process will get easier and become more natural
the more you do it.

REMEMBER
*There's no right way to do this exercise. There's only the
way that works best for you. Play around, have fun, and
try to figure out what is most helpful.*

PART II

CONNECT & COMMUNICATE

Now that we've walked you through a process for assessing and managing your worries, we want to give you the tools to assess how your kid is doing and what steps you can take to help them on their journey. Because when you get down to it, while we do our best to connect and communicate with our kids, sometimes it's downright difficult to gauge what's really going on.

Little ones don't always have the words to express how they're feeling, so they throw tantrums, bite, cry, or scream when something is upsetting them. Teenagers may refuse to interact with us precisely because we're their parents. To make matters worse, the pandemic made it very challenging for us to connect with the people we often rely on to help us assess how our kids are doing — their teachers, school nurses, guidance counselors, therapists, and friends.

As we've said before, you know your child best. Our goal is to provide you with sample questions and simple approaches you can adapt to help you connect with your kid and cope with the unique circumstances you find yourself in while also preparing them for the future. The most important thing to remember is that the best ways to help your kid involve listening when they want to talk and letting them know they are loved and safe.

Step 5: Establish a Baseline

Start by thinking about how your child has changed from their baseline. What are you accustomed to seeing from them in terms of their behavior? How does what you've seen recently differ from that?

Regardless of their age, there are some considerations we recommend you keep in mind when thinking about your kid's baseline:

Connections

- With their peers: Have they gotten more comfortable entertaining themselves, or do they seem bored? Have they stayed in touch with friends virtually? Are they asking when they can see their friends in person again?
- With you: Do they engage and interact with you or the rest of the family or mostly keep to themselves? Do they seem to crave your attention more now than they used to?

Energy Levels

- Do they seem to need more or less sleep now?
- Have their sleep and wake schedules shifted significantly?

Curiosity/Interest In Life

· Do they seem to have an active interest in activities or hobbies?
· Do they engage with the world or seem withdrawn?

Appetite

· Are they eating more or less than they usually do?
· Have you noticed any significant weight gain or loss?

MENTAL NOTE

If you've noticed significant changes in your child, they are most likely behaving in a new way because they're not fully able to express their feelings. These kinds of behavioral adaptations are often common among kids who are experiencing change in their lives. It's how their bodies let them know something is different or unusual. If you notice drastic changes in your child related to two or more of these areas that last over two weeks, it may be time to reach out to a professional for help to see whether or not therapy or another form of treatment could be beneficial.

Step 6: Know How and When to Connect

Before you start talking to your kid about how they're feeling and what this next phase might look like, take a moment to set the stage. Consider how you might respond to questions your kid is likely to ask. Think through what it feels like to be where you are right now, and then put yourself in their shoes.

See if you can tap into where you were mentally when this all began. Looking at the survey responses found in Appendix A could help jog your memory. Some of what you read might resonate with you or even sound like what you've heard your kid say during the pandemic. This perspective can help you prepare for how you want to approach the conversation with your kid.

DON'T MAKE A BIG DEAL OUT OF IT

In terms of finding a good time to talk, if you already have a time during the week or month when you talk to your kid about whatever's on their mind — maybe at Friday night dinner or during breakfast on the weekend — you may want to introduce this conversation then.

Sometimes making a point to schedule a time to talk gives kids more anxiety because they're anticipating it, whereas if you try to engage them in other everyday activities like when you're taking the dog for a walk or driving somewhere, you may find that the conversation happens more naturally. Your kid may even bring it up.

The key is to make sure your kid doesn't feel manipulated into having a conversation they don't want to have. Otherwise, they'll most likely approach it from a place of defensiveness, wondering why you didn't trust them enough to be direct about what you wanted to discuss.

You also want to make it clear that you respect your child as a thinking, feeling human being. Kids are often very clued in to what they can and can't say around you. They're most likely to be the least upfront with you about the things that may ultimately be the most concerning, so gaining their trust by proving you respect them is essential if you want to have a successful conversation.

TAKE IT SLOW

This is a process, and the conversation doesn't have to happen all at once. In fact, it may be easier to approach it in bits and pieces. See if you can help your kid warm up to the idea of sharing how they're doing, and then give them permission to put on the brakes. They may need to stop and digest what you've talked about or what they've realized while talking. Let them know they can steer the conversation and start and stop it based on how they're feeling.

BE HONEST

Consider how you want to let your child know that things won't be exactly like they used to be before the pandemic happened. While they may be going back to the same school and you may be going back to the same office, the experiences and the people in those places will not be the same. Everyone has been impacted by the pandemic in different ways. Preparing together for the changes to come is the best way to ensure a positive outcome.

It's also common for kids to be fearful or anxious about uncertainty. Here are some potential conversation starters that may help you think through how you want to approach your kid.

You've probably noticed how much things have changed throughout the pandemic, especially now that we're finally moving forward and getting out more. I'm guessing you and your friends are talking about this, and maybe you've seen some things on TV or online. You probably have some thoughts about this, too. Do you think you'd be willing to share a little bit about how you're feeling right now?

Another way to approach it might be to say: *Things seem to be starting to move in a new direction with the pandemic, and I'm wondering what it's going to be like, how we can manage it best, and what steps we can take to make it easier on all of us.*

The goal is to set a collaborative, honest tone.

BE OPEN

Once you've listened to what your kid has to say, you should feel comfortable sharing how you're feeling — as long as you don't lean on your child for support. Sharing your concerns should be followed up by sharing how you're coping with them. This helps your child understand they're not alone and that there are strategies for feeling better.

If you haven't addressed your own worries, your child may be concerned about going to you if they've noticed you seem upset or uneasy. They may think to themselves, *I don't want Mom or Dad to cry or get upset again, so I won't tell them that I'm worried.*

Try to stay calm when talking to your child, even if that means taking a moment or two to pause before responding to unexpected questions. It's okay to tell them you need a short break and step out of the room to collect yourself. Pause and tap into your breath. Go back to what we talked about in Part I. Then, when you're ready, jump back in where you left off.

HARD CONVERSATIONS MATTER

It's important to have challenging conversations like this, particularly during tricky transitions when most kids have a lot of questions (and much of the time they don't even know those questions are fueling their anxiety). Your child can get information from a lot of sources — their friends, neighbors, social media, and the internet. Sometimes what they hear is either a half-truth or just plain false. It's much better for them to hear the truth from you and know they can ask you about any questions on their mind in the future.

Your child will also feel safer and more connected to you when you talk to them about real concerns. You are modeling how to become more self-reliant and preparing them to learn how to constructively address their concerns as they grow up.

Step 7: Have Age- and Stage-Appropriate Conversations

Think about your child's age and where they are intellectually and emotionally to help you deliver the message in the most effective way. It's also critical to consider your child's individual personality and experiences before you begin.

If you have more than one child, try to talk to them separately so they have your full attention and they're more likely to be honest (as opposed to putting on a show for their siblings or trying to act "cool"). If possible, let their questions lead the conversation. Avoid offering a lot of additional information if they don't ask for it.

MENTAL NOTE

In general, younger kids are going to be much more influenced by you. They actively and openly seek connectedness with their parents — not to the exclusion of their friends, but their caregivers make up a big part of their orbits. The older they get, the more they begin to connect with their peers. We'll address this in more detail a little later.

In general, research suggests that the following guidelines may be helpful:

1. Be an Active, Engaged Listener

To really connect with your child, give them your undivided attention and let them talk. When you think they're done or ready to take a break, try repeating back what you heard to make sure you understand what they're trying to convey, show them you're listening, and validate their thoughts and emotions.

See if you can wait a few seconds longer than you normally would to jump in. If you're the one asking questions, try to give them the opportunity to think about their response (and even come back to you later, if they prefer). This takes some of the pressure off of them and helps them build self-confidence.

2. Ask Them What They Know

This will help you learn what information is missing or incorrect so you can try to give them a more accurate understanding of the situation. It's also a nice entry point for the conversation because it's pretty straightforward and doesn't immediately ask them to share their feelings.

3. Let Them Know Whatever They're Feeling Is Okay

Some kids feel pressure to act or feel a certain way because of peer or parental pressure. It's important to reassure them that all of their feelings are valid— even if they're conflicting, confusing, or scary. Emphasize that you're there to listen, not judge.

4. Recognize Your Biases

When you delve into a conversation like this, you may not always be aware of how biased your own point of view is. Spend a little time beforehand considering others' perspectives on the same topic. It's important to acknowledge there are always other sides to every story.

5. Offer Them Encouragement

Whether you give them a hug, kiss, or cuddle after the conversation or simply remind them they're not alone, try to offer them a sense of security and safety.

And while there are no firm rules when it comes to age-appropriate conversations, here are a few general guidelines that may help you think through your approach ahead of time.

LITTLE KIDS: AGES 4-8

Little kids don't really have a sophisticated understanding of logical thinking. They also have limited attention spans and absorb information primarily in small doses, so they have trouble understanding complex concepts. It can be helpful to break up difficult conversations into small chunks that you can then present one piece at a time. This gives your kid a chance to process each part separately. Younger kids may interrupt conversations to go back to play for a while and then come back to work through their thoughts later on. Making it clear that you're ready to listen when they're ready to talk gives them a sense of confidence.

1. Pay Attention to How Your Behavior Impacts Them

Children of this age are very sensitive to you as their caregiver and can easily be affected by your behaviors and your state of mind. You are one of their primary humans, so they may be much more aware of how you're feeling, thinking, or acting than you realize. It's important to understand that you can have an impact on them whether you intend to or not. They may misinterpret your behaviors or words. It's best to think through your ideas and feelings before you talk with your kid and reassure them that you can have reactions and opinions about issues but that they are always your first priority and that any stress or sadness you feel about events is not directed at them.

2. Help Them Express How They Feel

If they have trouble finding words to express their thoughts or feelings, follow their facial expressions or gestures and try to offer them words you think might fit to describe their feelings. For example, *Your frown is telling me that you are sad that you have to go back to school today after being home with me for a while. I understand that. I'm a little sad, too. What can we do to feel better? Would you like to bring a picture of us to school so you can look at it? That might help cheer you up until I come get you later in the day.*

3. Keep an Eye on Their Media Intake

You have more control over what they see and hear than you do with their older siblings, so do your best to expose them only to age-appropriate information.

MIDDLE SCHOOLERS: AGES 9-12

This age group is still coming to terms with what's pretend and what's real. As they get older, they start to be able to grasp more complex concepts. But they're also more likely to be exposed to information online that may be misleading or incorrect. And because they're starting to be more influenced by their peers (not to mention tweens are going through puberty), it's crucial that you create a protected space together where they know it's safe and okay to talk to you about how they're feeling or what they're experiencing without any embarrassment or shame. To reassure them, you can say things like, *No matter what you're feeling, I won't be mad. You can talk to me about anything, and we can figure it out together.*

1. Timing Is Everything

Kids in this age group are often quick to come talk to you if something upsets or scares them. Feel them out to see whether or not they want to keep talking.

2. Help Them Develop Critical Thinking Skills

Help them begin to think more in-depth about topics by asking questions beyond those that require a simple "yes" or "no" answer. Often giving a child a chance to answer in their own words can give you insights you would have otherwise missed.

3. Focus on the Positive

Try to stay as optimistic as you can so they know you haven't lost hope.

TEENAGERS: AGES 13-18

By now, your kid is starting to separate from you more — primarily engaging in conversations and activities with their friends. Chances are they're consuming media content on their own, engaging in what interests them and making their own tweets, GIFs, videos, or comments online. This is when they start to think they know best and don't want to be spoken down to (or even just talked to some of the time). Encourage them to do research on topics that interest them and then try to see if you can talk to them about it afterwards.

Teenagers often want an immediate answer to a question and can lose interest if there's too much of a delay before they get one, so see if you can put aside what you're doing to answer them with your full attention. If you can't step away from what you're doing at that moment, ask them if you can set aside a time when you can talk with them in the near future.

 MENTAL NOTE

Teenagers are hardwired to be socially conscious, more so even than adults. Social peer influences are 50 times more powerful than almost anything else. It's normal for them to be pulling away from you. One of their primary developmental tasks is individuation. That's why they tend to listen to the advice of their group of friends rather than listen to you as a parent. You are meant to have a vanishing influence on them because it's important for them to identify with their peers and begin to form their own identities.

1. Open Dialogue Works Best

Whatever they're thinking, they need to know they can come talk to you without fearing negative consequences. Try saying something along the lines of, *Even if we don't necessarily agree, I am very interested in and curious about what you're thinking.* This shows them that everyone doesn't have to agree about everything all the time, but that it's always worth talking about differing perspectives with the people they love.

You might want to ask about where they learned something or why they believe certain facts are true. Support their ideas and ask open-ended questions. This will provide insight into who they're talking or listening to and who they trust for information.

2. Acknowledge What You Don't Know

Some teens think their parents have all the answers, while others think their parents don't know anything. It's important for them to recognize that neither of these assumptions is correct. If a question you don't have the answer to comes up, tell your kid you don't know and suggest you both learn more. You may want to ask if they'd rather do their own research and then come talk to you or if they want to pursue it with you.

In this process, it can be helpful if you explain a bit about the concept of bias and how it can put a spin on a topic — and on their thinking — without them even knowing. Ask them what they think about bias and why they think some people tell stories more objectively than others, especially on social media. In this day and age, everyone has the power to be a storyteller. Helping your child learn how to differentiate between truth and fiction is a skill they'll use throughout their lives.

3. Problem Solve with Them

This age group may be more inclined to participate in a conversation when they feel like they have a say and can present their own ideas and opinions. Think about a scenario or two that you could ask them about beforehand, and see if they're willing to think through a solution with you. In addition to being a life lesson, it also helps empower them and gives them hope. Where there is potential, there is possibility. You can ask them about what they'd do if their friends dared them to take off their mask before they were vaccinated. Or maybe talk to them about whether or not it's safe to share food with friends at the lunch table. Whatever you think will be relatable to your kid is where you should start.

Step 8: Offer Reassurance, Love, and Support

Regardless of their age, it's important to reassure your child that even though what they've been through and are going through now may be scary or unsettling, you will figure things out together.

Part of reassuring your child is helping them acknowledge and express their emotions. Children and teenagers become more confident when they know they're not alone in how they're feeling, so be honest if you are scared or anxious too. Honesty and openness will also help build trust.

When facing new situations or when they feel unsafe or unsure, children need to know that their parents will always be there for them. Try to offer them comfort by reminding them that no matter how they're feeling, you will always love them. You can also reassure them by talking about specific, tangible steps you can take to help them feel safer.

There are many small but meaningful ways to remind your child how much you care. Make an extra effort to praise them when they share a toy or do well on a test. Do something special with them—play that game they've been begging you to play, or take them out to lunch during school. Give them a 'just because' hug, or send them a text that says, *You're awesome*. Read to them a little longer before bed, or ask them to play that song they've been practicing on the clarinet. Enjoy the simple act of sharing a special moment.

CONNECT & COMMUNICATE CHECKLIST

Why am I doing this again?

- It can be hard to know what's really going on with our kids, and the pandemic has made it even more difficult.
- The best way to learn how they're doing is to have honest, open conversations with them.

❑ Step 5: Establish a Baseline

Think through what you were used to seeing from your child before the pandemic and compare that to what you're seeing now. Consider their connections, energy levels, sleep/wake cycles, and appetite. If you notice drastic changes in your child related to two or more of these areas that last over two weeks, it may be time to reach out to a professional for help to see whether or not therapy or another form of treatment could be beneficial.

❑ Step 6: Know How and When to Connect

Decide whether you want to let them come to you or set a time to talk to them. Make it clear that they can stop and start the conversation based on how they feel. Eye contact and careful listening let them know you respect them and that you're available whenever they need you.

❏ Step 7: Have Age- and Stage-Appropriate Conversations

Communicate with your child on their level, age-wise and developmentally. Learn what they know. Let them know that anything they're feeling is okay. Share how you're feeling, and offer suggestions on what you're doing to address those emotions.

❏ Step 8: Offer Reassurance, Love, and Support

Change can bring up a lot of anxiety for kids. Help build their confidence by reassuring them through your words and actions, letting them know they are loved and safe. Come up with some small ways to remind them how much you care.

REMEMBER
When in doubt, always ask for help, whether you reach out to a friend, family member, or mental health expert.

PART III

PLAN & ACTUALIZE

Life rarely gives us the opportunity to reflect on how we've operated in the past and consider how we might be able to improve certain aspects of our lives. If ever there was a moment like that, this is it.

Before you start planning and going about your daily routines as the pandemic abates, consider pausing for a moment. Was there anything over the past year that brought you and your family closer together? How about your community? Did you find time to do things you hadn't made room for in your life before? Or did you cut out things you don't really miss now that they're gone?

Maybe your priorities and values have shifted, particularly in the way you parent and care for others. Maybe not. Either way, a lot has happened over the course of the pandemic. This is your opportunity to reexamine how you lived your life before and how you want to move forward.

It's also a nice opportunity to connect with your kids to see what—if anything—they'll miss about pandemic life. If they haven't already returned to school in person, they may have a lot of mixed emotions about what's to come in the fall. Taking the time to plan with them and prepare together will help make the transition to post-pandemic life easier.

Step 9: Consider the 'Old Normal'

There's no way around it — transitioning into the next 'new normal' is still going to have its challenges. It's helpful to be prepared for what it might bring up for you and your family. One way we suggest you begin this process is by setting aside a little time to think about your pre-pandemic lifestyle. What kinds of activities did you or your kids participate in before everyone's world was turned upside down? Were you primarily functioning on autopilot, or were you tuned in to how you were feeling and what was going on around you? Taking stock of how life used to be can help you think through what you want the future to look like.

Another suggestion is to go through the survey we included at the back of the book (found in Appendix A).

Here are the questions we asked kids from ages 4-18:

1. What are three words to describe how you feel right now?
2. When you think about going back out into the world, what things make you nervous or scare you?

3. In what ways have you seen people help each other during quarantine?
4. What are you most excited to do when this is over, or what are you most hopeful about for the future?
5. What do you think we could all do going forward to help make the world a better place once the virus is gone?

You can do this activity with your child, where you ask the questions and then the two of you write down and share your answers. Or, you can give your child the questions to answer on their own. Maybe they'll even be willing to share their answers with you later on.

If you want, you can revise a few of the questions to make them more relevant to our present situation:

1. What are three words to describe how you feel right now?
2. When you think about going back to the classroom/summer camp/birthday parties/ the community center, what things make you nervous or scare you?

3. What did you notice about how people helped each other during quarantine?
4. What are you most hopeful about for the future?
5. What do you think we could all do going forward to help make the world a better place?

Alternatively, you may want to create a list or chart with your kid of what the two of you liked and didn't like doing during the pandemic and what you want to take with you in the future.

All of these processes can help inform how you decide to build a new schedule together while also helping you reflect and process your experiences during the pandemic.

Step 10: Decide What Matters Most

It's also worth considering what you as a parent or caregiver want to model and what values and priorities you want to instill.

MODEL POSITIVE BEHAVIOR

During the pandemic, many of us realized how much our moods and emotions affected our kids, perhaps even more than we'd acknowledged beforehand.

To take stock of this, consider how and when you consume media. Do you have the TV or radio on all the time? Are you constantly checking your phone, or does it make a noise every time someone contacts you? See if you can find times when you can turn off your devices—especially during mealtimes or when you're all together as a family.

MENTAL NOTE

Even if the news is on in the background, your brain is operating based on a heightened level of alertness, so when it's no longer there, you unclench your mental muscles a bit. If you can't disengage, that's when it's time to turn it off for a while.

Sharing good coping skills for managing stress can also be helpful. If your kids see that preparing and eating healthy meals, exercising, and participating in calming or enjoyable activities make you happy or help you calm down, they're more likely to participate in these activities too. We've provided some additional resources you may want to check out in the back of the book (found in Where and How to Get Additional Support).

Everyone has days when they don't feel 100%, so during those times, consider asking yourself how you can demonstrate what it means to be a good, strong, adaptive person even when you're not feeling your best. You may want to share how you're feeling with your kid; let them know that emotions come and go, and then share what you're doing to manage those feelings or brainstorm with them about ways you can help yourself feel better. This teaches them how to communicate their feelings in a healthy, constructive way while also giving them solution-oriented approaches that can help them throughout their lives whenever difficult emotions arise.

EMBRACE UNCERTAINTY

As adults, many of us have come to terms with the fact that much in life is uncertain. We've learned tactics for living with an ever-evolving reality. To kids, however, feeling uncertain can be very disconcerting.

The best thing you can do for your kid to help them understand this somewhat complex concept is to first make sure you've developed your own level of comfort with it. Then you can demonstrate how to handle it for your kids. One key element to embracing uncertainty is being able to distinguish between what is and isn't in your control. By walking your kid through the process we discussed in Part I, you can provide them with a simple exercise they can use anytime they feel overwhelmed or anxious. Another part of teaching them how to overcome their fear of the unknown is to demonstrate how important it is to remain as flexible and open as possible.

 MENTAL NOTE

Helping your kid understand that each of us has the chance to make choices in our lives even when things around us are constantly changing can be empowering for them. It can be a little nerve-racking, but it can also embolden them to think about what kind of future they want and how they might go about creating it. When we understand that the world is evolving, we can build our capacity to adapt and remain steady in the face of challenges.

FIND TIME TO SPEND TOGETHER

Many of the children we heard from in our survey commented on how much they enjoyed spending more time with their parents doing activities during quarantine. This may be something they miss when they think about how life is changing. Make time to be together, whether it's looking at the stars while lying down on the front lawn, playing board games after dinner, or just sitting together on the couch.

If your child tends to dwell on what they wish they could be doing, consider making a wish jar. Every time they think of something they want to do when it's safe to be without masks or safe to travel, they can write it on a piece of paper and put it in the jar. Then they can pick wishes out of the jar when the crisis is over. This gives your child hope for the future, teaches them the value of delayed gratification, and reassures them that you value what they're thinking and feeling.

Step 11: Build a Better 'New Normal'

As you think through how you want life to be going forward, remember that all schedules require flexibility. If you schedule everything from the get-go, you're likely to get discouraged and overwhelmed (and discourage and overwhelm your family in the process). We suggest you start with two of the biggest activities in everyone's day: sleep and mealtimes.

We recommend you begin with these specific activities because they have a huge impact on your family's overall health and emotional well-being. Sleeping and eating habits often get out of whack when you're stressed or in crisis mode. So imposing a little structure on when you do those activities can help train your body to create healthier habits.

WHY SLEEP MATTERS

When it comes to your health, sleep is as important as eating, drinking, and even breathing. Getting your sleep back on track by setting and following through on specific bedtimes (regardless of whether it's the week or weekend) is critical for you and your child to get through this transition successfully. Without it, you'll find it's harder to concentrate and respond quickly in your daily life, and it can make it more difficult for you to process and retain memories.

MENTAL NOTE

A good night's rest gives our bodies time to repair themselves and our minds the chance to process and consolidate information. If you're not sleeping over a long period of time, it can wreak havoc on your body. Poor sleep is associated with physical problems, such as a weakened immune system, and can contribute to anxiety.

Between kids going to bed later because they don't have to get up to get ready for school and teenagers getting hooked on playing video games with their friends into the early hours of the morning, our sleep schedules have all been influenced in some way or another by the pandemic.

MENTAL NOTE

*When you think about sleep, you need to consider
bedtimes and wake times, but you also need to think
about bedtime routines. If you want somebody to
be able to go to sleep, you don't want to encourage
them to play video games right before it's lights out.
The blue light your phone emits stimulates your
brain and tricks it into thinking you're awake, which
doesn't help calm your or your child's brain down and
prepare it to sleep.*

*Start off by looking at what you and your kid are
doing on any given day before you go to bed. Maybe
you can track it on your phone or on a piece of paper
for a week. Then think about how their schedules
will change in the fall when they go back to school.
See if you can begin to get the family into a more
realistic routine sooner rather than later. If you wait
until the week before, you'll have to deal with this
adjustment at a time when your kid's emotions may
already be running high because they're nervous
about school restarting.*

WHY MEALTIMES MATTER

Making the time to eat well is also a fundamental component of good health and well-being.

 MENTAL NOTE

Healthy eating helps us maintain a healthy weight and reduces our risk of type 2 diabetes, high blood pressure, high cholesterol, cardiovascular disease, and some cancers. For many of us, this is old news. What we don't always hear about is how significantly good nutrition impacts our mental health too. Eating a well-balanced, healthy diet can help you focus, feel more alert, and improve your concentration and attention span.

Perhaps you started sitting down for a family meal once or a few times a week during the pandemic. If so, that may be a routine you want to continue so you have the opportunity to connect on a regular basis and check in with each other.

Meals are another great time to model positive behavior. Put your phone or other devices away so you can focus your full attention on your family. Ask your kids (and partner, if relevant) to do the same. They may be reluctant at first, but stepping away from the constant barrage of information can create a more peaceful environment for all of you. It's also a good time to see how everyone is doing. If your child brings something up that's concerning to you, try to talk to them about it either in the moment (if they seem open to talking) or at another point later in the evening or the next day. Only you know how urgent it is to talk about, so follow your instincts if it seems serious; don't put off having a hard conversation.

Keep the process simple. After all, you're going to be piloting this idea for a bit, and pilots have intervals — maybe you want to try the routine you come up with for a week or two. Schedules need time to work. If your family has decided to try eating dinner together, for example, give it a week and then check in with everyone to see how (and if) it's working. Although your kids may not be thrilled by the new plan (particularly if you have teens), if they show up and show some signs of engagement (they respond to your questions with more than one-word answers, they listen intently, you catch them smiling or laughing during a conversation), it means it's working and worth trying to continue the routine you've created for a while longer, if not permanently.

SETTLE ON SOME STRUCTURE

Before school starts (aka over the summer), it may be worthwhile to create a space at home that is similar to your kid's space at school. Creating a designated desk or workspace for your kids may help them focus, which is beneficial for everyone. You can do the same for yourself. But if you don't have room — you're all sharing the kitchen or living room, or multiple kids need to rotate using the computer so dedicating a space is out of the question — you can structure your day based on what kids normally do at school.

If you have a preschooler at home, try to follow the play-snack-rest model as best you can. With teenagers, creating "study halls" or gym class can help break up their day. Even having your kids get up and walk around like they would if they were changing classes every 50-60 minutes can be helpful. Moving your body often helps clear your head and allows you to refocus on the next task at hand. It can be as easy as taking the dog for a walk or going for a short jog. Throwing a ball around at the neighborhood basketball courts can also reduce some of the stress that's built up and creates a nice break in the day.

Consider writing the new schedule on a whiteboard and posting it somewhere in your house where your kids can see it so they know what's coming next (and so they won't ask you every five seconds). This helps them feel more in control of their lives, which can assuage their fears. It grounds them and helps them feel safe, as they can anticipate what is coming.

For many children (particularly children living with autism), structure represents safety; without it, they may flail or even emotionally collapse. A large segment of kids with or without autism don't like unpredictability, loud noises, boisterous people, or different smells and surroundings. They need to rely on something, and that something is a routine. Knowing what comes next means they can prepare for the transition in advance, which is comforting to many kids (and adults). It's also another way to help prepare your children to go back to school if they haven't already, which will undoubtedly make your life easier, too.

If your kids haven't gone back to school full time yet or have been on a hybrid schedule, consider talking to them about the transition by framing it in a way where you emphasize how much spending time together matters and how even though they'll be away from home more often than they have been, that doesn't mean there's less of a connection between the two of you.

You can let them know that going back to school and engaging with more people outside of the house are good things, you're proud of them, and you're there for them if they want to share how they're feeling. Explain that it's appropriate to have times when you go to work and school and then times when you're home with your family. This life lesson is another one that will stick with them for years to come.

PUT YOUR PANTS ON

If you haven't already, another way to structure your day is to start your morning the way you would have before the pandemic began. Get ready for your day as you normally would have (even if you're currently looking for a job, are working from home, will be transitioning back to the office, or are a full-time homemaker), and get your kids ready too (regardless of whether they're in the classroom, doing distance learning, or off for the summer).

MENTAL NOTE
The act of getting ready can actually lift you up mentally and physically. It lets your brain and body know things are in motion, which can help you be more productive as you move through your day.

MAKE SURE EVERYONE FEELS HEARD

Try to involve everyone so they feel empowered and included. This will help ensure that every family member feels a sense of ownership around the plan. For example, if your child suggests that everyone spend half an hour in the early evening one day a week before dinner playing catch and you decide to give it a go, they are more likely to show up ready to play because it was their idea.

We're not saying you have to agree to everything your child suggests. Kids sometimes have bad ideas, just like the rest of us. But see if there's a way you can work part of their suggestion into the plan.

LET THE PROCESS EVOLVE NATURALLY

Acknowledging to your kids that this is an evolving process and that you'll keep checking in with them about how the new plan seems to be going is helpful because it shows them that you value their input. This also allows for the flexibility you'll need when life inevitably gets in the way of your schedule or routine. Learning to be adaptable to a changing reality is a critical mindset to adopt and is especially useful for children as it will serve them for the rest of their lives.

As you well know, different approaches work best for different kinds of people. And different kinds of people often live under the same roof. One type may thrive on stimulation and attention. The other may really crave alone time. Both types are often exhausted by the other's lifestyle. So when thinking about a plan or schedule, consider how you can accommodate the different types of people in your family — the ones who lean toward active engagement and preoccupation versus the ones who lean toward independence and quiet reflection.

Set yourself up to be open to feedback from all of the members of your household, whether it's your 3-year-old, your 17-year-old, your parent, or your partner. All points should be considered as you work to create a schedule that works as well as possible for everyone, but don't change the plan every week. That will only create doubt, and your family may begin to lose hope that there's a plan you can all stick to. Instead, make a few adjustments at a time, as needed. Do the best you can with the feedback you get, and follow your instincts.

Step 12: Move Forward with Kindness

One of the most powerful takeaways from our survey was how focused kids of all ages were on being kind. Kindness isn't only something a 4-year-old understands, it's something they know how to do. They know concrete ways of showing kindness, and that's empowering for them.

A lot of the messaging in the world seems to be that everything is out of our control, so as you create your new plan, consider talking to your kids about how you might incorporate activities you can do and actions you can take as a family to show kindness toward others — whether it's donating food, serving at a soup kitchen, upping your recycling efforts, or lending a hand in the community. Being kind gives kids (and adults) a sense of accomplishment. It helps them cope by redirecting their energy, and it's also helpful from a developmental standpoint.

AUTHORS' NOTE

We hope this guide can help you and your family transition into a future all of you look forward to living. While many of the suggestions and tools offered are pertinent to the pandemic, we believe they're also applicable to any other big (or small) transition you may need to weather in the future.

Good luck on your journey. We're rooting for you all the way.

PLAN & ACTUALIZE CHECKLIST

Why am I doing this again?

- We can't control every aspect of our lives, but there are often small or significant changes we can make in how we spend our days that can help us live happier, healthier lives.
- It's helpful to be prepared for what this next phase might bring up for you and your family and to create a plan as you move forward.

❏ Step 9: Consider the 'Old Normal'

Think about your pre-pandemic life. What do you miss? What don't you miss? Consider going over the questions from the survey (found in Appendix A) with your kid or creating a chart or list of what you liked or didn't like about how life was before and during the pandemic.

❏ Step 10: Decide What Matters Most

Consider what values and priorities you want to instill. What kind of behavior do you want to model? How can you help your child learn to embrace uncertainty? Can you find ways to work quality time with your family into your schedule on a more regular basis?

❏ Step 11: Build a Better 'New Normal'

Start with ensuring healthy sleep and mealtimes. Remember the plan needs to be flexible and will evolve over time. Think about what other structure(s) might be helpful for your family. Make sure everyone feels like they have a say in the new plan.

❏ Step 12: Move Forward with Kindness

Kids of all ages understand what it means to be kind. Talk to them about concrete ways you can act with kindness toward others.

REMEMBER
How you decide to move into this next phase of your life with your family is up to you. There are no right answers, and no decisions you make today have to be permanent. Try to stay open and flexible, knowing that making the effort to create a plan is the best step you can take toward creating a smoother transition for everyone.

WHERE AND HOW TO GET ADDITIONAL SUPPORT

If you haven't contacted a mental health expert before, it can be an intimidating process. We've included resources to help you navigate your mental health services search. Much of this information was adapted from the Mayo Clinic, the National Alliance on Mental Illness, and the Mental Health America websites.

FOR EMERGENCY SITUATIONS

If you think your child could be a danger to themselves or others, get help immediately by calling 911 or going to your nearest emergency room.

Clearly state that this is a mental health crisis so the police or the ER nurse can handle the situation appropriately. Many communities have crisis intervention team (CIT) programs that train police officers to handle and respond safely to psychiatric crisis calls, so ask the 911 operator for a CIT officer, if possible. Your local emergency room is very familiar with crisis support situations. If you or your child is in the midst of a crisis, ERs have experienced people who can help guide you through the process of figuring out what to do.

FOR NON-LIFE-THREATENING CRISIS SITUATIONS

Different counties have different levels of crisis support — some even have drop-in crisis centers. You can contact your local ER, primary care physician's office, or outpatient therapist's office to get more information on these resources, or you can consult your county or city website. You can also go to findahelpline.com to identify the helpline(s) most applicable to your situation.

Alternatively, you can contact a 24-hour emergency crisis worker at the National Suicide Prevention Lifeline at 1-800-273-TALK (8255). The call, which is toll-free and confidential, will be routed to your nearest crisis center in the Lifeline network. You can also call 1-800-985-5990 or text "TalkWithUs" to 66746 at the SAMHSA Disaster Distress Helpline. It's best to identify these resources *before* a crisis so you have the numbers handy if you need them.

If/when you call, you'll be connected to a crisis worker who understands that this is a difficult call to make and will help you work through the immediate crisis and recommend next steps. Most offer triage, screening, preliminary counseling, and referral services. In extreme cases, they may refer you to the ER, offer to send a specialist to your home to help in-person, or arrange transport for psychiatric admission.

FOR GENERAL MENTAL HEALTH SERVICES

For more general information about mental health or to find mental health services or treatment options in your area, you can contact the Substance Abuse and Mental Health Services Association (SAMHSA) Treatment Referral Helpline at 1-877-SAMHSA7 (1-877-726-4727) during weekdays from 8 a.m.-8 p.m. You may also find it useful to check out the Child Mind Institute (childmind.org) as you continue to support your child's mental well-being.

If you have insurance, you may want to start by reaching out to your provider for a list of names of experts in and around your area.

If you don't have insurance, there are experts who can help you figure out how to get the services you need. You can reach out to a local services agency or a federally qualified health center, which is federally funded community-based healthcare. Most counties have a central office you can access through their website that coordinates all of the mental health services in your county. They can help you identify people you can talk to and work through payment and insurance challenges.

The bottom line: Always reach out to professionals if you're concerned. Asking for help is a sign of profound strength.

MORE RESOURCES

Telehealth mental health services saw a huge rise in popularity during the pandemic. There are many great options for meeting with professionals on a remote basis, which may make it easier for you to access the right care. One option is Little Otter,* a mental health care company centered around improving access to quality mental health care for kids and families. For more information, visit Little Otter's website (littleotterhealth.com).

There are a lot of meditation and mindfulness apps out there. Calm,* Headspace,* UCLA Mindful,* MyLife Meditation,* and Healthy Minds Program* are all free (and offer paid subscriptions for access to more content) and provide some combination of meditations, videos on mindful movement, sleep stories, calming music, and masterclasses from experts if you want to take a deeper dive. If you're interested in meditation specifically, you may want to check out Tara Brach's* guided meditations or podcasts (tarabrach.com).

If you want to start teaching your kids (and possibly yourself) how to be more present, you may want to look into Mindful Kids Cards by Little Renegades.* You and your child can pick a card at random and then follow simple mindful exercises that help both of you tap into basic techniques like awareness, breathing, meditation, gratitude, and stretching. Visit littlerenegades.com for more information.

If you're interested in advocacy work, we wholeheartedly support efforts to overcome mental health stigmatization. For more information on how you can help or get involved, consider checking out the resources provided on the National Alliance on Mental Illness website (nami.org).

*The authors have no business or financial connections with the company and resource suggestions.

NOTE: All information in this book, including resources, are suggestions for self-help steps and are not a substitute for medical advice or care.

APPENDIX A

WHAT WE LEARNED WHEN WE LISTENED

The following quotations and observations are based on a short survey containing five questions we invited parents and caregivers to talk over with their kids to help them get in touch with how they were feeling during the pandemic.

We reached out to as many families as possible with the help of friends and family, the University of Virginia's Multilingual Outreach Volunteer Effort (MOVE) program, nonprofits and community organizations, and social media platforms.

SURVEY SUMMARY

Even the littlest kids demonstrated a tremendous amount of social consciousness about the pandemic. They were very aware of the fact that they had to be protective of their grandparents as a vulnerable population, and they were dedicated to helping others to keep them safe. Some of them were worried about being a risk to other people, whether it was at school or around their families. For a 4-year-old, that kind of awareness is unusual, but given the realities of the situation, it's not necessarily surprising. The concern around this is that if kids are worrying all the time, their symptoms may progress into an actual anxiety problem, which could potentially lead to them needing professional treatment down the road. The best way to address this is to continue to check in with them regularly and ask for help if you're concerned.

When we asked about their fears, monsters and other imaginary threats came up a lot with the littlest kids, which is typical for this age group when they're worried. They talk about monsters because it's their best approximation of how to turn their worries into something more tangible. They can't compartmentalize or vocalize exactly what they're worried about; they just know they feel uneasy. It's a natural connection for them to associate their anxiety with something frightening in their world. The middle schoolers seemed to be unsure of what to think and how to feel. Many of them said they were tired, nervous, confused, or sad. These responses are fairly typical of this age group, as they are going through a developmental phase where they are trying to sort out what's happening in their bodies and in their minds. They were thinking about the logistics of going back out into the world, how that would impact school, and how people would socially distance and keep their masks on. They were also worried about spreading the virus, which was something the teenagers mentioned too.

What stood out in the late teen kids was a more personal focus, but not inappropriately so. They were concerned about how the pandemic was impacting their entry into college or their ability to get a job. The 2008 recession left a lot of young people with bad outcomes. Many of them lived with their parents for a long time because they couldn't get jobs; others went into debt. The current generation of teenagers seems concerned about similar bad outcomes — more worried about their fate and success than is probably typical. These kinds of concerns can put an inappropriate or undue amount of pressure on teenagers around adult concerns, which isn't entirely healthy for them.

**SURVEY WITH SAMPLING OF
ANSWERS BY AGE**

QUESTION 1: What are three words to describe
how you feel right now?

LITTLE KIDS (AGES 4-8)

- *Good, happy, and ready to work* (Cesare, 4)

- *Good, stinky, squishy* (Cecil, 4)

- *Happy-ish, bored, happy-bored* (Audrey, 4)

- *Happy, excited, energetic* (Isaac, 5)

- *Happy, frustrated, silly* (Lily, 6)

- *Happy about bike riding every day and no
  school; sad about the virus* (Archie, 7)

- *Tired, brilliant, mad* (Madeleine, 8)

- *Good, family-time, together* (Tzipi, 8)

MIDDLE SCHOOLERS (AGES 9-12)

- *Scared, happy (for being always with my family and for my mom being home and cooking dinner every night), and tired* (Adara, 9)

- *Nervous, confused, sad* (Finn, 10)

- *Unsure, bored, nervous* (Jo, 10)

- *Happy, content, and tired* (Jayden, 10)

- *Tired, lonely, sad* (Anon, 11)

- *Stuck, confused, and grateful* (Samantha, 12)

TEENAGERS (AGES 13-18)

- *Comfortable, energetic, happy* (Dan, 14)

- *Lonely, destitute, confused* (Jonathan, 15)

- *Annoyed, bored, disappointed* (Kenny, 15)

- *Lost, jumbled, and sad* (Kennedy, 15)

- *Happy, excited, silly* (Fiona, 17)

- *Safe, bored, antsy* (Sophie, 18)

QUESTION 2: When you think about going back out into the world, what things make you nervous or what scares you?

LITTLE KIDS (AGES 4-8)

- *That someone in my family will get sick* (Ben, 4)
- *Spooky monsters hiding in dark caves* (Cesare, 4)
- *Monsters* (Cecil, 4)
- *Nothing* (J, 4)
- *I might get eaten by a bear or a dragon, or you might get sick.* (Audrey, 4)
- *School* (Isaac, 5)
- *I'm scared about having to get the shot that they are working on.* (Finn, 5)
- *I don't want my family to get the germ bug and get sick.* (Lily, 6)
- *The coronavirus is going to be around for the rest of my life.* (Gus, 8)

◆ *That they don't stock the things I want at the store* (Gabe, 8)

◆ *People can still get the virus, and it will go on.* (Tzipi, 8)

MIDDLE SCHOOLERS (AGES 9-12)

● *Catching COVID and giving it to the ones I love; how sometimes people don't stay 6 feet away* (Adara, 9)

● *That our school will close and won't be able to survive because it is so small and already is struggling* (Mareana, 9)

● *I want a bunker and a hazmat suit.* (Finn, 10)

● *I'm less scared. I'm more just cautious, and if I stay that way then I feel I will be fine.* (Sadie, 10)

● *Having to wear a mask, what if it falls off, etc.* (Jo, 10)

● *Getting sick* (Anon, 11)

- *I think the only thing that scares me is just the fact that there is always a risk of another outbreak. There is always a chance that it is not totally gone, and then we might have to go back into quarantine, and I would hate for that to happen.* (Molly, 12)

TEENAGERS (AGES 13-18)

▲ *Getting the virus and giving it to other people* (Jonathan, 15)

▲ *Having all this happen again/getting sick* (Kennedy, 15)

▲ *The differences in people's behavior and people not acting the same around me* (Kenny, 15)

▲ *Not everyone doing their part and practicing safe distancing and wearing masks* (Sophie, 18)

QUESTION 3: In what ways have you seen people help each other during quarantine?

LITTLE KIDS (AGES 4-8)

- *Doctors helped us away from monsters* (Cecil, 4)

- *Wearing masks* (J, 4)

- *Sewing blankets and giving them to people who can't get up* (Audrey, 4)

- *Grandparents taking care of their grandchildren* (Isaac, 5)

- *I'm a hero by washing my hands after I pick my nose.* (Cy, 6)

- *We make masks for each other; we don't get close to other people, but we do nice things like drawing rainbows. We call people we love on FaceTime.* (Lily, 6)

- *Washing hands to stay safe* (Archie, 7)

- *We wear masks to try and not spread coronavirus if you have it.* (Madeline, 8)

- *Friends doing shopping for each other* (Elliott, 8)

- *Finding ways to connect remotely* (C, 8)

- *By delivering groceries to people who can't get it themselves* (Gabe, 8)

- *Packing food; calling people who are alone* (Tzipi, 8)

MIDDLE SCHOOLERS (AGES 9-12)

- *Less pollution by not using their cars; our neighbors have been helping us* (Adara, 9)

- *Someone made me a mask.* (Finn, 10)

- *Reminding people to wear masks and socially distance. We haven't really been going out a lot, so I haven't seen many examples of anything.* (Jo, 10)

- *Drop off food, and giving out masks, and helping educate on how to wash hands* (Jayden, 10)

- *Helping less fortunate people and giving to shelters and food banks* (Samantha, 12)

TEENAGERS (AGES 13-18)

▲ *Friends delivering food to others* (Dan, 14)

▲ *Donating money, donating food, creating new ways to bond; connect and replicate what we have to miss due to COVID. Also, less pollution!* (Kennedy, 15)

▲ *Making masks and sending them to others. Delivering food; sports players giving money to workers.* (Kenny, 15)

▲ *People getting and delivering supplies for loved ones, inspirational talks, and being there for one another* (Jonathan, 15)

▲ *Help brothers and friends* (Fiona, 17)

▲ *In my town, everyone has been wearing masks, which helps the community at large.* (Sophie, 18)

QUESTION 4: What are you most excited to do when this is over? What are you most hopeful about for the future?

LITTLE KIDS (AGES 4-8)

- *Visit my grandparents! I miss them so much. And go to the beach.* (Ben, 4)

- *Play days and eating a hundred cakes with my closest buddies!* (Cesare, 4)

- *Go to the children's museum and see the bugs!* (Cecil, 4)

- *Go to the bookstore and give hugs* (J, 4)

- *Do play dates* (Isaac, 5)

- *That this thing can stop so I don't have to wear a mask and not be stuck in the house. I'm excited to go to school, but I don't want to wear a mask.* (Madeline, 8)

- *To see my friends* (C, 8)

- *Everything, go to stores, candy stores. Hopeful for the future—that I don't die!* (Gabe, 8)

- *Squeeze my cousins and family; playing with friends without doing social distancing* (Elliott, 8)

MIDDLE SCHOOLERS (AGES 9-12)

- *Getting to spend time with my friends* (Mareana, 9)

- *We can go back to normal as soon as possible.* (Sadie, 10)

- *To go on trips to a different state* (Finn, 10)

- *I'm hoping that this will be over by the end of fifth grade so we can start going places again, especially summer camp. Seeing friends and going back to school. Going shopping, and swimming, and performing in theater again.* (Jo, 10)

- *Have a sleepover with my friends* (Jayden, 10)

- *Sports. There are no sports right now, and a lot of people like watching it or doing it.* (Sadie, 10)

- *I wish that we would grow from this and recognize how lucky we all are to be so healthy and okay. I wish people would stop taking that for granted and really just cherish the time they have with family.* (Molly, 12)

- *Be kinder to the earth, and respect each other more* (Luna, 12)

- *To see my friends and hang out without being worried about getting sick* (Samantha, 12)

TEENAGERS (AGES 13-18)

- *Play sports* (Dan, 14)

- *I'm most excited to go back to school and see all of the people I've lost touch with over the past couple months.* (Jonathan, 15)

- *That we will be able to maintain a respect for the small things in life, stay kind, and stay considerate* (Kennedy, 15)

▲ *Hanging out with friends again and having a good summer* (Kenny, 15)

▲ *Go to a restaurant* (Fiona, 17)

▲ *I am excited to hopefully have a normal college experience!!* (Sophie, 18)

QUESTION 5: What do you think we could all do going forward to help make the world a better place once the virus is gone?

LITTLE KIDS (AGES 4-8)

◆ *More time than anyone can imagine for love and playing...and more time with mommies for love* (Cesare, 4)

◆ *Hugs* (J, 4)

◆ *Helping! Helping people and animals — yay! Getting them food and just helping* (Audrey, 4)

◆ *Helping the world* (Isaac, 5)

◆ *Be nicer to each other all of the time.* (Lily, 6)

- *Don't litter; and never mix trash with recyclables.* (Archie, 7)

- *Help refugees by giving them clothing and school supplies and letting them live here.* (Madeline, 8)

- *Doing more planet saving as individuals — picking up other people's rubbish ourselves and spending more time with my family* (Elliot, 8)

- *MTWABP (make the world a better place) by picking up trash and helping people if they fall* (C, 8)

- *Hugging people* (Gabe, 8)

- *Be nice to each other.* (Tzipi, 8)

MIDDLE SCHOOLERS (AGES 9-12)

- *Start using bicycles or walking so that we stop polluting our environment; try recycling more things and reusing them.* (Adara, 9)

- *Wash your hands, stay safe, and even if there isn't a pandemic going on, you should still be cautious.* (Sadie, 10)

- *Spend more time with each other.* (Finn, 10)

- *Write thank you notes to all the nurses and doctors in the hospitals and to the people who work in grocery stores and people who are trying to help.* (Jo, 10)

- *Help clean the ocean and stop pollution.* (Jayden, 10)

- *Make sure to take better care of our older relatives (grandmother, grandfather) and do things to make their life easier.* (Anon, 11)

- *We can use this to really recognize how lucky we all are. If you look at how many people lost loved ones during this, we can use this to look back and really see how important it is to make sure that we spend as much time with family as possible before it's too late.* (Molly, 12)

- *Be kind to everyone, because everyone deserves a fair life.* (Samantha, 12)

TEENAGERS (AGES 13-18)

▲ *Rebuild the police* (Dan, 14)

▲ *Be more open and honest with each other because you never know when everything can change.* (Jonathan, 15)

▲ *Stay kind.* (Kennedy, 15)

▲ *Be thankful for what we have and not take anything for granted.* (Kenny, 15)

▲ *Be nice.* (Fiona, 17)

▲ *Be kind and inclusive to everyone in this world.* (Sophie, 18)

ACKNOWLEDGMENTS

We would like to thank our families for their ongoing encouragement and understanding. We are deeply grateful for your love and support throughout this process — and always.

This project would not have been possible without all of the parents and caregivers who completed the survey with their children. We cannot thank you enough for encouraging your kids to share their experiences of the pandemic with us.

Madelyn Fernstrom's enthusiasm and contributions made all the difference in turning this inkling of an idea into a reality. Lisa Medders' sharp eye and passion for mental health were instrumental to streamlining and fine-tuning this guide. Thank you also to our cover designer, Ceci Sorochin, and book designer, Lindsay Starr, both of whom eagerly jumped in to make this happen.

Thanks also go to Lauren van de Kamp, who championed this book again and again. We are grateful to Dr. Helen Egger and Rebecca Egger, the co-founders and CEOs of Little Otter, for their time and enthusiasm. A big thanks to Kelli Palmer, who helped us connect with leaders at numerous local nonprofit organizations to distribute our survey to a wider audience, including Mia Woods at the Boys & Girls Clubs of Central Virginia, Victoria McCullough at Sin Barreras, and Jon Nafziger at the Child Health Partnership. Alizé Dreyer and Elizabeth Wittner at the University of Virginia's Multilingual Outreach Volunteer Effort (MOVE) program enlisted their wonderful volunteers to translate the survey, making it possible for us to distribute it in multiple languages.

MeiMei Fox was kind enough to connect us with Leah Cotton and Jhanai Clark, both of whom volunteered their time and brainpower to move the project forward in addition to sharing the survey with their networks. Laura Moore helped think through how to get this project started and offered her insights as a school counselor.

Helen Patuck's book, *My Hero Is You*, was part of the inspiration for this guide, which began as a children's book. We also want to express our deep gratitude to Sabina Gault, Kathryn Hellwig Delbò, Valerie Harness, Sydney Chakalos, Stephanie Lovegrove Hansen (for the title, among other things!), Leilani Gushiken and the Gushiken Institute, Mary Gold, Dan Sheehan, Sarah DeSalvo, David Hazard, and Sarah Christensen Fu.

Guy Wilbur Fiske passed down his talent for storytelling, imagination and whimsy, for which Jacquelyn is deeply grateful. And a huge thank you to Jacqui and John Lazo, who always encouraged her to follow her passion for writing. Without them, she probably never would have imagined writing a book.

To everyone who supported us on this journey — our heartfelt thanks.

Made in the USA
Monee, IL
22 July 2021

73583063R00066